apocrifa

POEMS

* * *

Amber Flame

Red Hen Press | *Pasadena, CA*

Book Design by Mark E. Cull

Library of Congress Cataloging-in-Publication Data

Names: Flame, Amber, 1981– author.
Title: Apocrifa: poems / Amber Flame.
Description: Pasadena, CA: Red Hen Press, [2022]
Identifiers: LCCN 2022019298 (print) | LCCN 2022019299 (ebook) | ISBN
  9781636280639 (paperback) | ISBN 9781636280646 (ebook)
Subjects: LCGFT: Poetry.
Classification: LCC PS3606.L353 A76 2022 (print) | LCC PS3606.L353
  (ebook) | DDC 811/.6—dc23
LC record available at https://lccn.loc.gov/2022019298
LC ebook record available at https://lccn.loc.gov/2022019299

Publication of this book has been made possible in part through the generous financial support of Francesca Bell.

The National Endowment for the Arts, the Los Angeles County Arts Commission, the Ahmanson Foundation, the Dwight Stuart Youth Fund, the Max Factor Family Foundation, the Pasadena Tournament of Roses Foundation, the Pasadena Arts & Culture Commission and the City of Pasadena Cultural Affairs Division, the City of Los Angeles Department of Cultural Affairs, the Audrey & Sydney Irmas Charitable Foundation, the Meta & George Rosenberg Foundation, the Albert and Elaine Borchard Foundation, the Adams Family Foundation, Amazon Literary Partnership, the Sam Francis Foundation, and the Mara W. Breech Foundation partially support Red Hen Press.

First Edition
Published by Red Hen Press
www.redhen.org

Acknowledgments

Earlier versions of the following poems appeared in *Nailed Magazine*, an online literary journal, in February 2020: "cafuné," "*cinquain*: apprehension," "epistle: *a reply to friend still traveling*," "fernweh," "forelsket," "hyggelig," "naz," "onsra," "yuanfen."

An excerpt of "forelsket" was printed as a broadside and displayed in exhibit at Core Gallery in Seattle by Expedition Press in April 2018.

This book would not have been possible without time to write at Hedgebrook and the work of their librarian, Evie Long-Wilson, who gave me a stack of research bibles and articles on Solomon and the Queen of Sheba. The title and structure began to bloom with the loving first-reads of my Cranes, Kate Gray, Brionne (Breezy) Janae, Ruby Hansen-Murray, and Anna Vodicka. Early readers were instrumental in the story developing with these two characters, thanks to Elaina M. Ellis, Natasha Marin, Kristen Millares Young, and drea brown. The essential editing work of Sam Preminger was crucial to the intricate and exquisite exactness of every line, every poetic definition, every non-English word. His delicate touch and care made this book the precious and right thing it is. Thank you again to Kristen Millares Young, who introduced me to Tobi Harper. My unending gratitude to Tobi, who saw me, and Kate Gale, who saw this book as a thing of beauty and created space for it to be birthed.

dear reader, this is a spell for you. if you've been lonely, or broken. if you've longed for love that did not make you afraid to be whole. if you've longed to be free and longed to be home. if you've ever made your self a home for love or a perch from which love flies. dear reader, may this book be a sacred vow you intend for only true love's ear to hear.

Table of Contents

odic

English (adj.):

1. inspiring elaborate or irregular metrical form
2. emotionally exalted or enthusiastic

the words that propel this love story
are borrowed from across the world,
& do not lend to a direct translation.
all attempts at definition are taken
with poetic license & great respect.

voorpret

Dutch (n.):

1. physical excitement in anticipation of fun or pleasure
2. the first sweet awareness

elegy: **solitude**

once sure of everything:

a youngling,
a ripe plucking.

eaten
before fruit rotted,
letting juice wander
of its own will.

when my ache finds me, i

am perpetually sticky,
drawing bees.

certain
the cycle of drupe, of all
things fertile; sure consumption
is the way to reap a harvest.

toska

Russian (n.):

1. the anguish of both melancholy and ennui
2. a great hunger with no satisfaction

i, always
distant star
measureless sea
untilled field

discover
my wandering
has left me
an arid heart
salted throat.

epistle: *a postcard upon arrival*

greetings from _____!

i have made it safely, and how wonderful
it is to look forward to this lovely bed
and delicious food at day's end!
i'm in no rush to move on.
perhaps constant motion
is not the dream,
after all . . . it is quite beautiful
here as you can see, and—dare
i say it—this might be the place
for me
to put down some roots.
oddly, i do feel i am missing
home—
whatever that's supposed to be.
no promises!
but i'm likely to be
here
awhile.

quatern: **premonition**

here is a home i built myself,
the foundation strong, unmoving
soil familiar as my skin;
all paths lead me back here.

solitude, my own well-worn cloak.
here is a home i built myself
to toil for and rest within—
a haven, a completed pride,

to make friends of moist morning grass,
the hearthfire and rising breadloaf.
here is a home i built myself:
nothing lacking, no need to roam

for company—all life outside
my door beckons wonder and awe!
i am surfeit, calm content, in knowing
here is the home i built myself.

yuanfen

Chinese (n.):

1. a meeting caused by fate
2. an inexorable interaction with no destined outcome

animal me can taste
you coming. how
bone popped
crackling staccato
jaw in slow
stretch;
teeth unsheathing.

the puncture;
hip and rib
threaten
skin.

your smells on my tongue
lay thick in wait.

mamihlapinatapei

Yagan (n.):

1. seduction without explicit action
2. the act of waiting for the other to initiate contact

in the gardens,
a flowering vine;   you, plump tendril
overgrown.

i linger.

in the city,   you, overdue guzzle
an overfull cup to slake;

palm the curve
of me and be pleased.

koi no yokan

Japanese (phrase):

1. a long-awaited premonition
2. someone who fits the fantasy of love

i offer sugared
smile,

all slippery
fingers,

and pulp-stained love notes.

a guileless offering.

a craving
expressed in sweet wet.

my mouth, full,

a flood,
tissue insides
giving way to

urgent

scissoring teeth.

with hunger pangs

belly
a taut esurience.

gretchenfrage

German (n.):

1. what are your real intentions?
2. an essential question with a difficult or dubious answer

lover, you are   a precipice

steep drop

blood rush.   genesis,

are you

a cessation?

                                        yes.

fensterln

German (v.):

1. gain entry through surreptitious design
2. accept the lure of an open, yet lofty entrance

gluttonous lover,
i am eager, a

i will not curb my tongue;
merchant of the honeyed mouth.

here,
an open window where i am drawn
at midnight. you

clumsy leap.
slicked lips sing
siren up over
edges.

join with me at breath.

kilig

Tagalog (n.):

1. irrational behavior due to overwhelming emotion
2. erratic actions due to strong feelings of fear or want

i, twitching skin
bristled follicle

        while awaiting
        a kiss,

forget to sleep

        blurred eyes
        focus

sudden awake
to greet you

        on threshold;
        home.

iktsuarpok
Inuit (n.):

1. one who impulsively goes outside to check and recheck whether a lover has arrived
2. the sweet anticipation and exquisite ache of waiting

before you
i am stripped
unashamed,

these fingers
make your breath
fistful. live wire,

compulsively clutching.

a cavern gulping
for tide.

hold, my love,
the wave crests yet.

forelsket

Bokmål (v.):

1. catch one's breath in throat when thinking of a lover
2. experience mundane life overtaken by euphoric glow

each day now,
everyone scents me
primed. obtainable.
flushed husk.

reassure them: it is wonder.
the sun, all the stars.
how they shine so brightly.

sapped bones.

beloved, overgrown tongue.

we begin:
eyes brimming with each other,
bruised mouths

swollen in greeting.

covenant
of wet and blood.

naz

Urdu (n.):

1. arrogance in being the object of one's affection
2. the surety of feeling completely adored

lover calls me space and sky—
charts constellations
across my limbs.

your touch, the sun's noonday heat
        on skin, dark and lovely and

in my thirst, i draw near—

suckle.

quench.

return.

in this terrain of riches
i am oceanic.

epistle: *a reply to a friend still traveling*

dear _____,

thank you for these
pictures! what a breathtaking view
—i've always wanted
to go exploring
there. tell me more!
how long
are you traveling?
where
do you go next?
fill me in on all your exploits!
i fear
love
makes a domesticated pet
of me.

cafuné

Brazilian Portuguese (n.):

1. the act of fondling the head or neck intimately
2. an entangling of fingers in a lover's hair

spin me your dreams.
curl your distant
longing round my thighs,

you, fallen
for the roadmaps
of my skin.

answer this:

i seek
adventure
in your hair's
tangled vines.

will i be

mouth nomad;
you, oasis pooling

where you go

sinking with every rise

?

hyggelig
Danish (adj.):

1. warm and comfortable demeanor
2. home-like

my unlatched garden gate
a ready welcome

—i make comfort
a dish to satisfy,
make steadfast
an elixir for your throat

you open, i rise

to sip from the
round bowl
of your navel

yet in my gullet
remains a
scratching.

hot.
not sated.

oodal

Tamil (n.):

1. an inconsequential lovers' quarrel
2. one who pouts after a fight with a partner

the embers
of my hearth
await your breath, yet

yesterday you were   a resolute glow,
a window.

                                       beloved, at ease.
                                       i, abandoned.

today
i find you replacing your   walking paths
                                       still seeking

laces.

luftmensch

Yiddish (n.):

1. one who dreams instead of being present
2. an air person

i chose you,

a whole desert in my teeth.

my thirst whistling,

still,
i chose you
despite desiccation.

fernweh

German (n.):

1. pain at the idea of staying home
2. home made in strange, unattained places

how you hold me
unwilling. how
bones ache there,

without the dampness
from rain:
without any particular
brokenness:

empty
where your marrow
should be.

i offer my pillow tonight,
beloved. you are pleasing and

warm.

does it matter
where i may go
while just now i rest
between your feet?

cinquain: **apprehension**

and what

should i make of

parting with no promise?

you and i never drew shackles

of love.

epistle: *a letter upon arriving in a new place*

beloved, did you see the big bright
moon last night? did i imagine
you at your garden's gate,
tracing its silver path
through the trees of your dear forest?
it loomed so large
as i watched it set from the train,
and i missed your warm
fingers entwined in mine.
love, the way the stars stretch
in this sky! i am learning constellations
i've never seen before. i cannot
wait to explore caverns
and mountains—perhaps i'll take a trip
down the river that snakes
through the valleys here. today,
i packed a lunch
to bring with me.
i sit in this meadow
munching fresh apples;

i am thinking of you.
i hope you are keeping
warm and well,
my love.

dor

Romanian (n.):

1. hurt that comes from separation
2. a person feeling physical pain from wanting

tarry yet
here with me, in

love, an uncut path.

shade's too-long tendrils

lack, a briar patch

—a risk i will call belief,
name hope.

la douleur exquise

French (phrase):

1. a heart that aches because it does not receive the love it longs for
2. one who wants to be loved in return, but is not

you found me
wing-ridden,

a bed of spices.

now, there are foxes
in my vineyards;

my head fills with dew.

and i drew near, as if

offered flight,

with all the world still
to taste.

kara sevde

Turkish (phrase):

1. a blinding zeal for another
2. that which darkens or blacks out reality

sustenance sours between my teeth;
a careless swallowing.

who has come to
unlock these gates?

my ribcage, an abandoned
storehouse—

sick with love.

for you,
the honey of my regard,
a constant offer.

i do not wish you a hollow knocking,
an unanswered invitation.
be replete;

tonight there is a feast of stars

dapjeongneo

Korean (n.):

1. a question where the answer is induced
2. one who baits the other into saying what they want to hear

shall i be fecund
or barren?

shall i be fecund
or barren?

shall i be fecund
or barren?

shall i be fecund
or barren?

shall i be fecund
or barren?

shall i be fecund
or barren?

shall i be fecund
or barren?

prozvonit

Czech (v.):

1. abandon contact before the other person can answer
2. save oneself from consequence by abruptly ending contact

i cannot love you enough
to unlove the wide world.

golden shovel: **laceration**

to
unlove
my own precious stem, the
undigging a wound wide
enough to birth you the world.

epistle: *a letter with a promise after*
receiving no response

dearest, oh, the wonders
in this world!
each place is its own marvel
—i feel my eyes devour
like mouths whose thirst
cannot be slaked.
there is nowhere life
does not bud,
thrumming
its everyday song.
yesterday the dawn greeted
me at water's edge
as i watched fishing boats
and gulls
begin their dance.
i am at peace, my heart,
yes, and you
are still the only
one
named home.

sestina: intention

what is it i can offer?
a bed for your bones
a refuge, warm;
does it matter
if you will not rest,
if you prefer empty?

my house is never an empty
cup. desire this host's offer:
a place of sustenance, rest,
and my delight in your very bones.
a place where you matter
and our bed is always warm.

now you grow lukewarm
a promise emptied
is no laughing matter.
what, then, will you offer
to re-flesh my bones,
to resolve this unrest?

where is the rest
of you, when i come to warm
each one of my bones
in a hearth now empty
of every flame you offered?
tell me i still matter.

do i still matter?
will i be left the rest,
the remains of an offering;
you, a warm
regard replaced with empty
belly, with skin and bones?

can i forget how traced bones
were all that matter
-ed, not the plates we left empty
or the bed we fell into, rest
-less and fevered. you, warm
and i, an always open offer

return. offer me back your bones.
warm to me again, you are the matter
of all my rest, you fill my empty home.

saudade

Portuguese (n.):

1. a desolate longing
2. wistfulness for what is lost

why sew
a garden with salt,

i,
an elapsed dream
consumed

tears souring
the very stone of the fruit

make meal of remembering

where there was sweet
ripe, spilling over.

onsra

Bodo (n.):

1. one who feels bittersweet about a love affair that won't last
2. one who is loving for the last time

what has become
of your caravan of treasure?

where once a full cup,
wine and milk.

aril of pomegranate.
crush of honeycomb.

a jealous doubt
takes root.

do not name me thief.

razliubit

Russian (n.):

1. someone who elicits tender memories
2. love's emptiness

doubt, a lazy
temptation,

who can forgive oneself
for the folly of love,

makes no effort at the burn

and leaves its mark

while still sipping
the scalding broth
of its torment

cavoli riscaldati
Italian (phrase):

1. a mess made while attempting to make something obsolete new
2. something unable to reignite once burned

no ash-choked hearth,
sapped vessel,

i, a rebuilt wall,
compost my regard.

a patient backbone.
my hands, seedlings.

neither desert
nor sacrifice—

who would desire
a vacant lot of your soil

you, beloved, all a riotous bounty.

lítost

Czech (n.):

1. one who unexpectedly realizes they are the source of their torment
2. sudden miserable insight into oneself

my mind grows weary
treading fearful waters
visions half-formed
and ill-truthed
and so i surface, gasping

believe this prize
of a vagabond heart

in its flux
an innervated thrilling
trills this request:

i covet our bed;

return to me
your brightness.

make your arms adit again

epistle: *a journal entry pondering return*

i count the steps still
between us with questions
left me. the sky, an omen
of rain. have you learned
to believe in me, dearest?
have you put away my chair?
or filled it with a new lover?
will you bestir your heart anew?
am i your eidolon,
still welcome?
and what has taken seed
in my absence?

viraag

Hindi (n.):

1. a sense of emotional folly due to alienation
2. an absurd estrangement

what absence
could unlearn my palms
the way to knead breadloaf,

could sap greening
from my fingertips

and is your heart not
more steady

did i not know its constance
as we lay, my ear pressed
to its chamber?

what forgetfulness

or new adventure call

could erase the direction
of haven

media naranja

Spanish (phrase):

1. the half that betters the whole
2. one who feels incomplete or bisected

long loneliness
carved valley
of my chest

remind me
hold my own mouth
wide.

overflown banks,
broken levies past

instruct my course
a boundless outline;

it rains, beloved.

sonnet: **inhalation**

today, the dead thing on the forest path
as i walked to the tree where we first met
did not immediately bring regret
did not burn through my empty chest as wrath
it was, after all, a thing whose time passed.
who mourns each night because the sun has set?
i know bones and flesh are simply the debt
the earth always comes to collect at last.
and here it was, all the sweetness greening.
i relearned how to breathe in deep relief
a world that continues even through grief,
even through what seems to have lost meaning.
as i walked, i saw nothing that stays dead—
just stasis, bud, blossom, fruit, repeated.

ilunga

Tshiluba (n.):

1. an imperfect person loving what one can tolerate
2. one who decides to try again when loving has failed

i remain my own self

wiser perhaps

but open

i remain my own self

less brash

expansive

in beloved's
sure regard

unceasingly free.

retrouvailles

French (n.):

1. one who salvages joy from reuniting
2. the feeling of reassembling one's fragments

at last!

my eyes

savage

and you

a feast.

this skin-starved collision

exhilarated

rapture

bitter made sweet again

epistle: *a note at the start of the day*
containing a conjuration

a peculiar fascination;
a lead with no collar; drawn to tongue
unfamiliar lexemes: shelter, hearth.

i am sure of your steady brilliance;
my own wax wane cyclic.
shall i be your best refraction?

love, station my orbit.

ode: **invocation**

be it fevered hope

        or of temporal stuff,

do not lure me

        from my lover's side.

o, do not keep from me

        the curving ridge and plane

        of rachis and shoulder blade,

let me tarry here;

        exquisite dip of hipbone

        and argil of thigh.

let me chart paths

    of this flesh.

    this flesh. all hill and hollow.

    this flesh.

let me sink

    and surface.

    let me linger. let me.

    hold. fast.

ya'aburnee

Arabic (n.):

1. someone who cannot endure the pain of living without their other
2. intention to not outlast love

anticipatory

i am eager harbor

for my

odyssean lover

beloved

i sojourn, merely.
no longer a quest

horizon-hunger

finds secure berth

apocrifa
Late Latin (n.):

1. that which is sacred; neither shunned nor shamed
2. an urgent gospel of love, a hymn in its name

Biographical Note

Amber Flame is an interdisciplinary artist whose work garnered residencies with Hedgebrook, Vermont Studio Center, and more. Her first poetry collection, *Ordinary Cruelty*, was published through Write Bloody Press. Flame is a recipient of Seattle Office of Arts and Culture's CityArtist grant and served as Hugo House's 2017–2019 Writer-in-Residence for Poetry. Flame's work featured in *Alone Together: Love, Grief, and Comfort in the Time of COVID-19*. She is Program Director for Hedgebrook, a residency for women-identified writers. Amber Flame is a queer Black dandy in Tacoma, Washington, who falls hard for a jumpsuit and some fresh kicks.